Imprint:

Copyright © 2013 GRIN Verlag
Print and binding: Books on Demand GmbH, Norderstedt Germany
ISBN: 9783656699538

This book at GRIN:

https://www.grin.com/document/276616

Tapan Gondaliya

Intrusion Detection System in mobile ad hoc network in MAC layer

GRIN Verlag

GRIN - Your knowledge has value

Since its foundation in 1998, GRIN has specialized in publishing academic texts by students, college teachers and other academics as e-book and printed book. The website www.grin.com is an ideal platform for presenting term papers, final papers, scientific essays, dissertations and specialist books.

Visit us on the internet:

http://www.grin.com/

http://www.facebook.com/grincom

http://www.twitter.com/grin_com

Intrusion Detection System in mobile ad hoc network in MAC layer

A Dissertation submitted

By

Gondaliya Tapan Pravinbhai

To

Department of Computer Science & Engineering

In partial fulfillment of the Requirement for

the

Award of the Degree

of

Master of Technology in Computer Science & Engineering

(April 2013)

ABSTRACT

The rapid proliferation of Mobile ad hoc network has changed the landscape of network security. The recent DOS attacks on major Internet sites have shown us, no open computer network is immune from intrusions. The ad-hoc network is particularly vulnerable due to its features of open medium, dynamic changing topology and cooperative algorithms, lack of centralized monitoring and management point and lack of a clear line of defense. The traditional way of protecting networks with firewalls and encryption software is no longer sufficient and effective.

In this work, an intrusion detection system will be developed for detection and isolation of attacks. IOn this research work, mac layer applications will be used for detecting malicious activities and will focus on the finding of attack sequences in the network. This research work will provide stable and effective attack observations which can be directly applicable to the Real environment for Mobile Ad-hoc Devices.

There are many intrusion detection techniques have been developed on Ad hoc network but have been turned to be inapplicable in this new environment. Here we need to search for new architecture and mechanisms to protect Mobile Ad hoc network. In the above all technique of intrusion detection is applied on the only one layer and that is probably on routing layer. But here we apply this intrusion detection system in the MAC layer for the more security, efficiency and high speed compare to other technique those whose apply in the network layer.

ACKNOWLEDGEMENT

First of all I would sincerely thank to my revered guide and mentor, Mr. Maninder Singh (Assistant Professor, Computer Science and Engineering Department, Lovely Professional University) for his valuable guidance, closely supervising this work over the past four months and helpful suggestions. His valuable advice and support, in spite of their busy schedule have really been an inspiration and driving force for me. He has constantly enriched my raw ideas with his experience and knowledge.

I would also heartily thank Mr. Dalvinder Singh, Head, Computer Science and Engineering Department who providing me lots of terms, technology and devices and providing a different kind of the seminar regarding to my thesis work and always very helpful and constructive.

Words are inadequate to express my heartfelt gratitude to my affectionate parents who have shown so much confidence in me and by whose efforts and blessings I have reached here.

I find it hard to express my grateful to the almighty in words for bestowing upon me his deepest blessings and providing me with the most wonderful opportunity in the form of life of a human being and for the warmth and kindness he has showered upon me by giving me life's best.

I wish to express heartiest thanks to my friends and colleagues for their support, love and inspiration.

Date: Gondaliya Tapan

                                                                                              Reg.No.11106452

3

TABLE OF CONTENTS

I. Declaration...

II. Approved Research Topic..

III. Abstract..

IV. Certificate..

V. Acknowledgement ....

VI. Table Of Content..

VII. List Of Figures ....

VIII. List Of Abbreviations ....

Page No.

Chapter 1. Introduction 10-24

1.1 Mobile Adhoc Network...10

   1.1.1 History of Mobile Adhoc Networks..11

   1.1.2 Overview Of Mobile Adhoc Networks..11

   1.1.3 Adhoc Routing Protocols for MANET...12

      1.1.3.1 Table Driven Protocols...13

          ⁃ Destination-Sequenced Distance-Vector Routing (DSDV) 14

          ⁃ Cluster head Gateway Switch Routing (CGSR) 14

          ⁃ Wireless Routing Protocol (WRP) 14

      1.1.3.2 On demand Protocols...15

          ⁃ Ad-Hoc On-Demand Distance Vector Routing (AODV).............15

          ⁃ Dynamic Source Routing (DSR)....................................15

      1.1.3.3 Hybrid Protocols...16

          ⁃ Zone Routing Protocol...16

1.2 Overview of intrusion detection...17

1.3 Intrusion Detection System...18

   1.3.1 Host based intrusion detection system..19

   1.3.2 Network based intrusion detection system...20

1.4 Why we need IDS..21

1.5 IDS Techniques...21

   1.5.1 Anomaly Detection..21

   1.5.2 Misuse Detection or Signature Detection...22

   1.5.3 Target Monitoring...23

   1.5.4 Stealth Probes...23

1.6 Overview of wormhole attacks..23

Chapter 2. Review of literature 25-34

Chapter 3. Present work..35-37

    3.1 Scope of Study 35

    3.2 Problem Formulation 35

    3.3 Objective 36

Chapter 4. Research Methodology 36

Chapter 5. Result and Discussion 38-47

Chapter 6. Conclusion and Future works..48-48

Chapter 7. References..49-51

LIST OF FIGURES

Figure No.	Name of Figure	Page No.
1.1	PRNET Architecture	11
1.2	Mobile Adhoc Nodes in MANET	12
1.3	Classification of Routing Protocols	13
1.4	Workflow of CGS Routing	14
1.5	Zone Based Routing	16
1.6	IDS Activity	17
1.7	IDS Types	19
1.8	A Typically Anomaly Detection System	22
1.9	A Typically Misuse Detection System	22
1.10	Wormhole Attacks	24
4.1	Tools Used	37
4.2	NS-2 Real Environment	38
4.3	NS-2 Simulated Environment	38
5.1	Compile the TCL File Successfully	39
5.2	Screen Shot of Run Time Screen	40
5.3	Screen Shot 10 Activate Nodes	41
5.4	Screen Shot of Moving Activate Nodes	42
5.5	Wormhole Attacks Between 3 Nodes	43
5.6	Automatic Activated Of IDS	44
5.7	Screen Shot of Packet Dropping	45
5.8	IDS Tried To Solved the Problem	46
5.9	Wormhole Attack Effect Decreases	47
5.10	Mobile Nodes In Its Normal Position	48

LIST OF ABBREVIATIONS

IDS	Intrusion Detection System
HIDS	Host Based Intrusion Detection System
NIDS	Network based Intrusion Detection System
DNS	Domain Name System
FTP	File Transfer Protocol
RDMS	Relational Database Management System
ZBIDS	Zone Based Intrusion Detection System
MANET	Mobile Ad Hoc Network
AODV	Ad Hoc Distance Vector
MIDS	Mobile Intrusion Detection System
MAC	Media Access Control
DOS	Denial Of Services
ARP	Address Resolution Protocol
RARP	Reverse Address Resolution Protocol
ICMP	Internet Control Messaging Protocol
IP	Internet Protocol
TCP	Transmission Control Protocol
UDP	User Datagram Protocol
DNS	Domain Name System
SMTP	Simple Mail Transfer Protocol
HTTP	Hyper Text Transfer Protocol
FTP	File Transfer Protocol
ZRP	Zone Routing Protocol
DSR	Dynamic Source Routing
AODV	Adhoc On demand Vector Protocol
WRP	Wireless Routing Protocol
CGSR	Cluster Head Gateway Switch Routing
DSDV	Destination Sequenced Distance Vector

Chapter 1
INTRODUCTION

1.1   Mobile Adhoc Networks

Mobile Ad Hoc Network (MANET) is a whole wireless connectivity through the various nodes constructed by the actions of the network, which has a basically dynamic shape and a limited bandwidth as well as topology is change. Mobile Ad Hoc Network (MANET) is a bunch of two more nodes or devices or terminals with wireless connectivity and networking capability that communicate with each other without any centralized administrator also the wireless nodes can dynamically form a network to exchanging information without using any occurrence of fixed network infrastructure. And it's an autonomous system in which mobile hosts connected by wireless links are free to be dynamically and some time act as routers at the same time.

There are three types of MANET. It includes Vehicular Ad hoc Networks (VANETs), Intelligent Vehicular Ad hoc Networks (InVANETs) and Internet Based Mobile Ad hock Networks (iMANET). VANETs are used for communication between two or more moving vehicles or between vehicles and fixed roadside equipment. Internet Based Mobile Ad Hoc Networks (iMANET) link mobile nodes and fixed Internet-gateway nodes. Intelligent vehicular ad hoc networks (InVANETs) help vehicles to behave in intelligent manner during vehicle-to-vehicle collisions, accidents, and drunken-driving.

Mobile Adhoc Network has a dynamic nature and is short of centralized stations as monitor stations, the ad hoc networks are vulnerable to various kinds of attacks. Mobile Adhoc network also suffered from vulnerabilities inward from wired communication systems like spoofing, eavesdropping, denial of service, authorization, access control. They also vulnerabilities ensuing from the wireless medium like wormhole, sinkhole, black-hole, sleep deprivation. Ad hoc routing protocols have vulnerabilities that also go ahead to fresh attacks on MANET systems.

1.1.1 History of Mobile Adhoc Networks

Earliest MANETs were called as a packet radio networks PRNET that is   sponsored by Defense Advance Research Project Agency (DARPA) in 1970. This packet radio network predated the Internet and was part of inspiration of the original IP suite, after that DARPA experiments built-in the Survivable Radio Network (SURAN) project in 1980s.

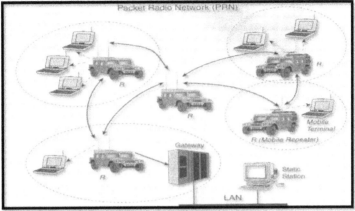

Figure 1.1 PRNET Architecture [6]

In 1990s the advent of inexpensive 802.11 radio cards for personal computer. Current Mobile Adhoc Networks are designed primary for military utility for examples include JTRS (Joint Tactical Radio System) and NTDR (Near-Term Digital Radio).

1.1.2 Overview of Mobile Adhoc Network

Manet is the Self-configuring network of mobile routers and also associated with the hosts connected by wireless links. Mobile Adhoc Network has union forms of random topology; one of the main issues of the mobile Adhoc network is ttopology changes rapidly and unpredictably. Standalone fashion or connected to the larger Internet. MANETs are self contained; they can also be tied to an IP-based global n/w as well as local network it is called Hybrid MANETs. Routes between nodes may potentially contain multiple hops and in first part of the figure nodes act as routers to forward packets for each other or in second figure contains node mobility may cause the routes change.

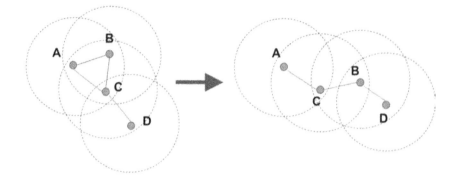

Figure 1.2 Mobile Adhoc Nodes in MANET [6]

Mobile Adhoc Network is Suitable for military conflicts, emergency medical situations, and emergency situations like natural or human-induced disasters.

1.1.3 Routing protocols for MANET

Routing Protocol in Mobile Adhoc network is mainly divided in to three parts one is table driven protocols and second one is source initiated on demand driven protocols and last but not least hybrid protocols that both protocol has its own importance and this protocol is also further divided into other protocols.

Table driven protocol it is also known as the proactive protocol. In table driven protocols continuously assess the routes and also attempt to maintain consistent, It also up-to-date routing information from routing table as well when a route is needed. Whenever the n/w topology changes the protocol respond by propagating updates throughout network to maintain a constant view. Example of this type of protocol is DSDV, CGSR, and WRP.

The second protocol of the routing mobile Adhoc network is on demand protocol which is also known as the reactive protocol. This protocol is maintain routes only if needed. Example of this type of protocol is AODV and DSR.

Last but not least the hybrid protocol is the third type of mobile Adhoc network protocol which is a combination of the both protocol on demand and table driven protocols example of this type of protocol is ZRP. Now let we briefly discuss all protocol as under.

10

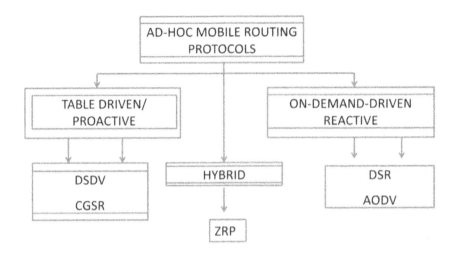

Figure 1.3 Classification of Routing Protocols in MANET [6]

1.1.3.1   Table Driven Protocols

Table driven protocol it is also known as the proactive protocol. In table driven protocols continuously assess the routes and also attempt to maintain consistent, It also up-to-date routing information from routing table as well when a route is needed. Whenever the n/w topology changes the protocol respond by propagating updates throughout network to maintain a constant view. Example of this type of protocol is DSDV, CGSR, and WRP.

- **Destination Sequenced Distance Vector (DSDV)**

Destination Sequenced Distance Vector is a table driven protocol, it is basically work on the Based on the distributed Bellman-Ford routing algorithm. In this protocol each node maintains the routing table. Mainly in this type of protocol is used for the control the traffic over the network two types of the route updates packet used for maintain the traffic over the network full dump and incremental in incremental packet Only information changed since the last full dump and in the full dump all available routing information. In routing table store the data like sequence number or the source to destination route information.

11

- **Cluster-Head Gateway Switch Routing (CGSR)**

CGSR is also the table driven protocol or proactive protocols in this protocol uses DSDV as an underlying protocol and least Cluster Change (LCC) clustering algorithm. Clustering is used as a able to control a group of ad-hoc hosts. In this protocol each node maintain two tables in it one is a cluster member table, containing the cluster head for each destination node and second one is a distance vector-routing table, containing the next hop to the destination

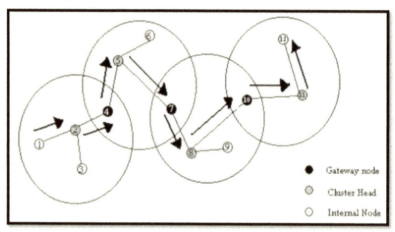

Figure 1.4Work Flow of Cluster Gateway Switch Routing (CGSR) [6]

One main drawback of this protocol is too frequent cluster head selection can be an overhead and cluster nodes and Gateway can be a bottleneck

- **Wireless Routing Protocol (WRP)**

WRP is also the proactive table driven protocol main goal of that protocol is maintaining routing information among all other nodes in the adhoc network. Each node contains basically 4 tables distance table, routing table, message retransmission list table or last link cost table. In this protocol link exchanges are propagated by using update messages sent between neighboring nodes, also the hello messages are periodically exchanged between neighbors node. Main problem solving out this protocol is count-to-infinity problem by forcing

12

each node to check predecessor information. Draw backs of that protocol is each node contains a 4 table and store lots of information so used large amount of memory is used and periodic hello message consumes power and bandwidth.

1.1.3.2   On Demand Routing Protocols

The second protocol of the routing mobile Adhoc network is on demand protocol which is also known as the reactive protocol. This protocol is maintain routes only if needed. Example of this type of protocol is AODV and DSR.

- **Ad hoc On-demand Distance Vector (AODV)**

AODV is a reactive type of protocol which is builds on DSDV algorithm and the improvement is on minimizing the number of required broadcasts by creating routes on through an on-demand. This protocol need the broadcast is used for route request, broadcast not maintaining a complete list of routes. Main Advantages of that protocol is responsive to changes in topology, uses bandwidth efficiently, is scalable as well as ensures loop free routing. And a drawback of that protocol is nodes use the routing caches to reply to route queries. Result: "uncontrolled" replies and repetitive updates in hosts' cache cannot prorogate the early response so all query messages which are flooded all over the network

- **Dynamic Source Routing (DSR)**

DSR is another protocol has a reactive type and which is basically working on concept of source routing. Mobile nodes are required to maintain route caches that contain the source routes of which the mobile is aware two mechanisms is used in this protocol Two mechanisms one is Route Maintenance and second one is Route Discovery Route discovery is uses the route request and route reply packets Route maintenance is uses the route error packets and acknowledgments. Main advantages of that protocol is no periodic hello message and fast recovery - cache can store multiple paths to a destination and one drawbacks of that protocol is the packets may be forwarded along stale cached routes Major scalability problem due to the nature of source routing.

1.1.3.3   Hybrid Routing Protocols

Last but not least the hybrid protocol is the third type of mobile Adhoc network protocol which is a combination of the both protocol on demand and table driven protocols example of this type of protocol is ZRP.

+ **Zone Routing Protocol (ZRP)**

Zone base routing protocol is the mixture of the above both of the protocols proactive as well as active. In this protocol proactively maintains routes within a local region or it is also called routing zone. All nodes within hop distance at most d from a node X are said to be in the routing zone of node X. All nodes at hop distance exactly d are said to be peripheral nodes of node X's routing zone. Also in ZRP a globally reactive route query/reply mechanism available.ZRP basically consist 3 protocols Intrazone Routing Protocol (IARP), Interzone Routing Protocol (IERP), Bordercast Resolution Protocol (BRP)

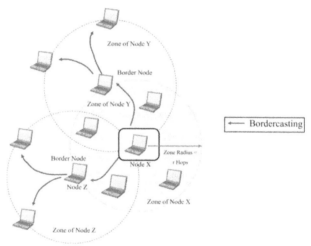

Figure 1.5 Zone Base Routing [6]

14

1.2   Overview about the IDS

Now a Days Hacking and intrusion incidents are increasing year by year as technology grow up. Unfortunately in today's inter-connected e-commerce world there is no hiding place: you can be found through a wide variety of means: DNS, Name Server Lookup, NSlookup, Newsgroups, web site trawling, e-mail properties and so on.

Whether the motivation is financial gain, intellectual challenge, espionage, political, or simply trouble-making, you may be exposed to a variety of intruder threats. Obviously it is just common sense to guard against this, but business imperative.

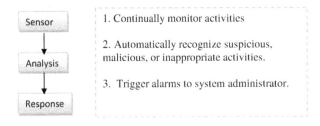

Figure 1.6 IDS Activity

IDS do exactly as the name suggests: they detect possible intrusions. More specifically, IDS tools aim to detect computer attacks and/or computer misuse, and to alert the proper individuals upon detection. An IDS installed on a network provides much the same purpose as a burglar alarm system installed in a house. Through various methods, both detect when an intruder/attacker/burglar is present, and both subsequently issue some type of warning or alert. Also IDSs may be used in conjunction with firewalls, which aim to regulate and control the flow of information into and out of a network; the two security tools should not be considered the same thing. Using the previous example, firewalls can be thought of as a fence or a security guard placed in front of a house. They protect a network and attempt to prevent intrusions, while IDS tools detect whether or not the network is under attack or has, in fact, been breached. IDS tools thus form an integral part of a thorough and complete security system. They don't fully guarantee security, but when used with security policy, vulnerability assessments, data encryption, user authentication, access control, and firewalls, they can greatly enhance network safety.

IDS have a 3 security functions: they 1.monitor, 2.detect, and 3.respond to unauthorized activity by company insiders and outsider intrusion. Intrusion detection systems use policies to define certain events that, if detected will issue an alert. In other words, if a particular event is considered to constitute a security incident, an alert will be issued if that event is detected. Certain intrusion detection systems have the capability of sending out alerts, so that the administrator of the IDS will receive a notification of a possible security incident in the form of a page, email, or SNMP trap. Many intrusion detection systems not only recognize a particular incident and issue an appropriate alert, they also respond automatically to the event. Such a response might include logging off a user, disabling a user account, and launching of scripts.

1.3   Intrusion Detection System

Intrusion detection system is a collection of techniques that are basically used to detect suspicious activity both at the network and host level. Intrusion detection systems fall into two basic categories: signature-based intrusion detection systems and anomaly detection systems. Intruders have signatures, like computer viruses, that can be detected using software. You try to find data packets that contain any known intrusion-related signatures or anomalies related to Internet protocols. Based upon a set of signatures and rules, the detection system is able to find and log suspicious activity and generate alerts. Anomaly-based intrusion detection usually depends on packet anomalies present in protocol header parts. In some cases these methods produce better results compared to signature-based IDS. Usually an intrusion detection system captures data from the network and applies its rules to that data or detects anomalies in it.

Basically the intrusion detection is the technique of monitoring networks for unauthorized entrance, activity, or file modification in network. IDS can also be used to monitor network traffic, thereby detecting if a system is being targeted by a network attack such as a Dos attack. There are two basic types of intrusion detection: HIDS and NIDS. Each has a distinct approach to monitoring and securing data, and each has distinct advantages and disadvantages. In short, host-based IDSs examine data held on individual computers that serve as hosts, while network-based IDSs examine data exchanged between computers.

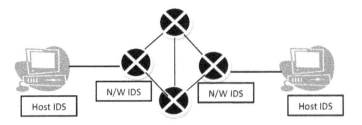

Figure 1.7 Types of the IDS

1.3.1 Host-Based IDS (HIDS)

HIDS were the first type of IDS to be developed and implemented. These types of systems collect & analyze data that originate on a computer that hosts a service, such as a Web server. Once this data is aggregated for a given system, it can either be analyzed local or sent to a separate/central analysis machine. Example of HIDS is programs that operate on a system and receive application or operating system audit logs. These programs are broadly effective for detecting insider abuses. On the trusted network systems them, they are close to the network's authenticated users. If one of these users attempts unauthorized activity, host-based systems usually detect and collect the most pertinent information in the quickest possible manner. In addition to detecting unauthorized insider activity, host-based systems are also effective at detecting unauthorized file modification.

On the down side, host-based systems can get unwieldy. With several thousand possible endpoints on a large network, collecting and aggregating separate specific computer information for each individual machine may prove inefficient and ineffective. In addition, if an intruder disables the data collection on any given computer, the IDS on that machine will be rendered useless because there is no backup.

Possible host-based IDS implementations include Windows NT/2000 Security Event Logs, RDMS audit sources, Enterprise Management systems audit data (such as Tivoli), and UNIX Sys log in their raw forms or in their secure forms such as Solaris' BSM.

17

1.3.2 Network-Based IDS (NIDS)

As Opposite side to monitoring the activities that take place on a particular network, NIDS analyzes data packets that travel over the actual network. These packets are examined and sometimes compared with empirical data to verify their nature: malicious or benign. Because they are responsible for monitoring a network, rather than a single host, NIDS tend to be more distributed than host-based IDS. Software, or appliance hardware in some cases, resides in one or more systems connected to a network, and are used to analyze data such as network packets. Instead of analyzing information that originates and resides on a computer, network-based IDS uses techniques like "packet-sniffing" to pull data from TCP/IP or other protocol packets traveling along the network. This surveillance of the connections between computers makes network-based IDS great at detecting access attempts from outside the trusted network. In general, network-based systems are best at detecting the following activities:

- **Unauthorized outsider access**: When an unauthorized user logs in successfully, or attempts to log in, they are best tracked with host-based IDS. However, detecting the unauthorized user before their log on attempt is best accomplished with network-based IDS.

- **Bandwidth theft/denial of service**: These attacks from outside the network single out network resources for abuse or overload. The packets that initiate/carry these attacks can best be noticed with use of network-based IDS.

- **Some possible downsides to network-based IDS**: include encrypted packet payloads and high-speed networks, both of which inhibit the effectiveness of packet interception and deter packet interpretation. Examples of network-based IDS include Shadow, Snort! Dragon, NFR, Real Secure, and Net Prowler.

1.4 Why We Need IDS

These attacks may consist of otherwise authorized users who are disgruntled employees. The remainder comes from the outside, in the form of denial of service attacks or attempts to network infrastructure. Intrusion detection systems remain the only proactive means of detecting and responding to threats that stem from both inside and outside a corporate network.

Intrusion detection systems are an integral and necessary element of a complete information security infrastructure performing as "the logical complement to network firewalls." IDS tools allow for complete supervision of networks, regardless of the action being taken, such that information will always exist to determine the nature of the security incident and its source.

Clearly, corporate America understands this message. Studies show that nearly all large corporations and most medium-sized organizations have installed some form of intrusion detection tool [SANS01]. The February 2000 denial of service attacks against Amazon.com and E-Bay (amongst others) illustrated the need for effective intrusion detection, especially within on-line retail and e-commerce. However, it is clear that given the increasing frequency of security incidents, any entity with a presence on the Internet should have some form of IDS running as a line of defense. Network attacks and intrusions can be motivated by financial, political, military, or personal reasons, so no company should feel immune. Realistically, if you have a network, you are a potential target, and should have some form of IDS installed.

1.5 IDS Techniques

There are four basic techniques used to detect intruders: anomaly detection, misuse detection (signature detection), target monitoring, and stealth probes.

1.5.1 Anomaly Detection

Designed to uncover abnormal patterns of behavior, the IDS establishes a baseline of normal usage patterns, and anything that widely deviates from it gets flagged as a possible intrusion. What is considered to be an anomaly can vary, but normally, any incident that occurs on frequency greater than or less than two standard deviations from the statistical norm raises an eyebrow.

Update Profile

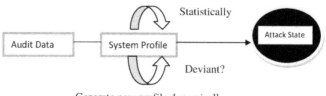

Generate new profile dynamically

Figure 1.8 A Typical Anomaly Detection System [1]

1.5.2 Misuse Detection or Signature Detection

Commonly called signature detection, this method uses specifically known patterns of unauthorized behavior to predict and detect subsequent similar attempts. These specific patterns are called signatures. For HIDS, one example of a signature is "three failed logins." For NIDS, a signature can be as simple as a specific pattern that matches a portion of a network packet. For instance, packet content signatures and/or header content signatures can indicate unauthorized actions, such as improper FTP initiation. The occurrence of a signature might not signify an actual attempted unauthorized access. But it is a good idea to take each alert seriously.

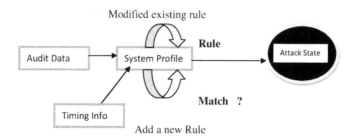

Figure 1.9 A Typically Misuse Detection System [1]

1.5.3 Target Monitoring

This type of technique does not actively search for misuse, but instead look for the modification of specified files or data. This is more of a corrective control, designed to uncover an unauthorized action after it occurs in order to reverse it. One way to check for the covert editing of files is by computing a cryptographic hash beforehand and comparing this to new hashes of the file at regular intervals. This type of system is the easiest to implement, because it does not require constant monitoring by the administrator. Integrity checksum hashes can be computed at whatever intervals you wish, and on either all files or just the mission/system critical files.

1.5.4 Stealth Probes

This type of system attempts to detect any attackers that choose to carry out their mission over longer periods of time. Attackers, Example, will check for system vulnerabilities and open ports over a two-month period, and wait another two months to actually launch the attacks. This system collects a broad-variety of data throughout the system, checking for any methodical attacks over a long period of time. They take a wide-area sampling and attempt to discover any correlating attacks. In effect, this method combines anomaly detection and misuse detection in an attempt to uncover suspicious activity.

1.6 Overview of wormhole Attacks

Wormhole Attack in Manet is one of the effective attacks on routing protocols in which two or more malicious nodes receive packets at one point of the network and transmit them to another location by a wired or wireless tunnel. This attack is very powerful and that the detection of it is very difficult work. This attack is a one kind of a serious threat in wireless networks, especially against many wireless ad-hoc networks and location-based wireless security systems. There is several wormhole detection and Prevention methods in the wireless ad-hoc networks some of them are described in this article [25].

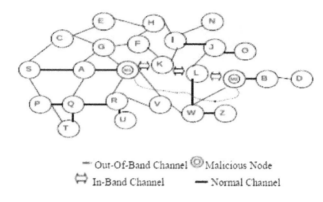

— Out-Of-Band Channel ◎ Malicious Node

⇔ In-Band Channel — Normal Channel

Figure 1.10 wormhole attacks [25]

There are some of the technique are define here Distance and location Based: Packet Leash Technique, Special Hardware Based Approaches, Localized Encryption and Authentication Protocol (LEAP), Topological Technique, Watchdog Technique, DelPHI Technique

Chapter 2
REVIEW OF LITRATURE

2.1 Introduction

This chapter contains the summary or conclusion about the different paper or also some of the important facts which will be used in this current paper. This paper is based on the other Intrusion detection systems

In the research paper Network Traffic Monitoring Using Intrusion Detection System, (January 2012) IDS have been to blend the use of pattern matching, stateful pattern matching. The IDS arena and will incorporate new techniques as they become efficient, practical, cost-effective, and commercially viable. Host based intrusion detection involves not only looking at the network traffic in and out of a single computer, but also checking the integrity of your system files and watching for suspicious processes. Network traffic monitoring is an analysis and reporting tool. It works in all Windows based operating systems. It captures all traffic transport over both Ethernet and WLAN networks. Network traffic monitoring decodes all major TCP/IP protocols. With Network traffic monitoring, you can easily filter the network traffic to focus on the information that you are looking for. Comprehensive reports and graphic views allow you to understand network performance and usage quickly and identify problems in simple steps. Protocol decoders for TCP/IP and many application protocols including ARP/RARP, ICMP, IP, TCP, UDP, DNS, POP3, SMTP, IMAP, HTTP/HTTPS, TELNET, FTP. Powerful and easy to set filters allow user to focus on useful traffic and narrow down the problem. [1]

According to Intrusion detection model (1987) Intrusion Detection System should be able of detecting all type of attacks which might be present in the network area. Security violations can be detected by monitoring system's audit records for abnormal patterns of system usage IDS should be capable to detect all type of attacks present on the network. Sometimes a false positive alarm in IDSs is occurred which is raised incorrectly. A lot of efforts have been made to reduce number of false alarm in intrusion detection system. [2]

Research paper of Zone-Based Intrusion Detection for Mobile Ad Hoc Networks, A general intrusion detection agent model and propose a Markov Chain based anomaly detection algorithm. Here protection of MANET routing protocols and present the details regarding feature selection, data collection, data preprocess, Markov Chain construction, classifier construction and parameter tuning. We demonstrate that local detection alone cannot achieve desirable performance. Therefore, we further propose a collaboration mechanism among ZBIDS agents and an aggregation algorithm used by gateway nodes. With alert information from a wider area, gateway nodes' IDS can effectively suppress many falsified alerts and provide more diagnostic information about the occurring attacks.

This paper presents the design of a non overlapping Zone-Based Intrusion Detection System (ZBIDS) for MANETs. We present details of constructing the Markov Chain based local anomaly detection model, including feature extraction, data preprocess, detection engine construction, and parameter tuning. Our simulation results demonstrate that the local anomaly detection model works well in low mobility environment. With high mobility, the local detection model and the aggregation algorithm under the zone-based framework should complement each other to form an effective and complete MANET IDS. [3]

This description is about the survey paper of Intrusion detection in mobile ad hoc network (2006) in this we classify the architectures for intrusion detection systems (IDS) that have been introduced for MANETs. Current IDS's corresponding to those architectures are also reviewed and compared. Although the watchdog is used in all of the above IDS, the authors in have pointed out that there are several limitations. The watchdog cannot work properly in the presence of collisions, which could lead to false accusations Moreover, when each node has different transmission ranges or implements directional antennas, the watchdog could not monitor the neighborhood accurately. All of the above IDS's presented are common in detecting nodes. However, CORE doesn't detect malicious misbehaviors while the others detect some of them, i.e., unusually frequent route update, modifying header or payload of packets, no report of failed attempts, etc. [4]

Regarding to paper of Distributed Intrusion Detection Models for Mobile Ad Hoc Networks (2002) basically developed four intrusion detection models which can be integrated with each other to become a complete intrusion detection system for MANETs.

Intrusion detection models for OLSR and AODV are representatives of proactive and reactive routing protocols in MANETs, respectively. The third is DEMEM, a fully-distributed message exchange framework designed to overcome the challenges caused by the decentralized and dynamic characteristics of MANETs. Last is DRETA, which utilizes cryptographic techniques to protect message integrity and authenticity. These four models working together can precisely detect anticipated routing attacks in OLSR and AODV, with low message and computational overhead. Furthermore, they also can be applied to secure other routing protocols in MANETs. [5]

Intrusion Detection System in Mobile Ad hoc Network (July 2008) Paper proposed IDS, referred to as MIDS, for wireless networks. MIDS can detect if nodes are getting their fair share of the transmission channel. It also detects packet drops or delays that violate the respective flow requirements. MIDS rely on overhearing packet transmissions of neighboring nodes that makes it an effective system in networks where nodes use different transmission power and directional antennas for different neighbors. MIDS does not require setting up various thresholds manually; rather it can select them dynamically. In future we want to implement all the causes of ATTACK1 and ATTACK2. [6]

In this paper of Power-Aware Intrusion Detection in Mobile Ad Hoc Networks Basically through GP program to know or the detect route or flooding disruption attacks against AODV and also implemented on the network architecture with varying mobility and traffic levels. We used both single fitness functions and multiple fitness functions. We have shown how in some circumstances a multiple objective approach provides a more effective means of searching the tradeoff space. Main work is unusual in that we trade off security performance (detection and false positive rates) against resources (power). It is likely that for some types of networks (e.g. sensor networks) the ability to make good tradeoffs will be particularly important. Our techniques can be used to generate solution sets with the best (or near best) tradeoffs possible. [7]

In this research paper of Evolutionary design of Intrusion Detection Programs proposed the establishment of an Intrusion detection Program which is basically detect known attack patterns. An IDP does not eliminate use of any preventive technique but it is work on the last defensive technique in securing the system. There are three variants of genetic programming mechanism namely Multi-Expression Programming (MEP), Linear Genetic Programming (LGP) and Gene Expression Programming (GEP) were evaluated to design Intrusion detection program. Some of the indices are used for difference between the detailed analysis of MEP technique is provided. Empirical results disclose that genetic programming technique could perform a main role in developing Intrusion detecting programming, which are light weight and accurate when compared to some of the conventional intrusion detection systems based on machine learning paradigms.[8]

In this research paper of Selective Jamming/Dropping Insider Attacks in Wireless Mesh Networks describe various types of unique attacks launched from adversaries with internal access to the wireless mesh network. Here also further identify possible detection and prevention mechanisms. The routing protocols in mobile ad hoc network mean that the mobile nodes will search for a route or path to connect to each other and share the data packets. The open nature of the wireless medium leaves it vulnerable to jamming attacks. Jamming in wireless networks has been primarily analyzed under an external adversarial model, as a severe form of denial of service (DoS) against the physical layer. Existing anti-jamming strategies employ some form of spread spectrum (SS) communication, in which the signal is spread across a large bandwidth according to a pseudo-noise (PN) code. However, SS can protect wireless communications only to the extent that the PN codes remain secret. Insiders with knowledge of the commonly shared PN codes can still launch jamming attacks. [10]

In this article of Wormhole Attack Detection in Mobile Ad Hoc Networks describe about the wormhole attacks, one malicious node tunnels packets from its location to the other malicious node. Such wormhole attacks result in a false route with fewer. If source node chooses this fake route, malicious nodes have the option of delivering the packets or dropping them. It is difficult to detect wormhole attacks because malicious nodes impersonate legitimate nodes The wormhole attack is possible even if the attacker has not compromised any hosts and even if all communication provides authenticity and confidentiality. In this paper analyze wormhole attack nature in ad hoc and sensor networks and existing methods of the defending technique to detecting wormhole attacks without require any hardware devices. This technique able to provide in generate a method to reduce the rate of refresh time and response time faster than first. [11]

In this research paper of "Securing Data in Ad hoc Networks using Multipath routing" discussing about the solution for how to securing data in ad hoc networks. Here utilize the exists of multiple paths between nodes in an ad hoc network to increase the strongly of transmitted data confidentiality. In ad hoc n/w, security depends on different parameters and getting a good security degree is a hard task. There are several proposed solutions authentication, availability, secure routing and intrusion detection system etc, in ad hoc networks. Briefly discussing of some current solutions, implementation parts and experimental results are described in this paper. [12]

In this paper of "Detecting Sinking Behavior at MAC and Network Layer Using SVM in Wireless Ad hoc Networks" Defines that Autonomous IDS which is using SVM. These feature set are constructed from Media Access Control layer and Network layer contains the normal behavior and malicious behavior of wireless node. In training data consist both of normal & abnormal behavioral patterns. Proposed system identifies both anomaly and Misbehavior of nodes in the network. Simulation is done under different n/w conditions and malicious node behavior. In that IDS The Data is analyzed through trace log. These feature values obtained are generated by simulating wireless node behavior and used by which SVM to detect intrusions. In this paper also define that AODV is an on-demand routing protocol. The AODV algorithm gives an easy way to get change in the link situation. For example if a link fails notifications are sent only to the affected nodes in the network. This notification cancels all the routes through this affected node. [13]

In this research paper of "Verifying Physical Presence of Neighbors against Replay-based Attacks in Wireless Ad Hoc Networks" consists verify the physical presence of a neighbor node in wireless ad hoc n/w is one of the most important parts in established protocols flexible to replay-based attacks. Here first consider the RTT-through verification and revise it along with a probabilistic approach. Here also they consider a power-based approach and connecting it with RTT-based approach to design an effective neighbor verification protocol (NVP). Using some of the real experiments, in this research they supposed the ideas and eliminate the impractical solutions. In this proposed protocol significantly limits the effectiveness of replay-based attacks by restricting the range where they might be launched and thus makes such attacks practically impossible. [14]

In this paper of "Transmission Time-based Mechanism to Detect Wormhole Attacks" Describe the different important apps of Wireless Ad Hoc Networks make them very attractive to attackers; therefore more and more research is requisite to assure the security for Wireless Ad Hoc Networks. In this paper also described, a transmission time based mechanism (TTM) to detecting wormhole attacks – that attack is one of the most powerful & serious attacks in WANET. Transmission time based mechanism detects wormhole attacks during route setup procedure by computing transmission time between every two successive nodes along the established path. Wormhole is identifying base on the fact that transmission time between two fake neighbors created by wormhole is considerably higher than that between two real neighbor nodes which are within radio range of each other. This technique has given the good performance, little overhead and no special hardware is required. It also creates unicast route from source node to destination node and that's why the network usage is least. Since the routes are build on demand so the network traffic is minimum. AODV uses Destination Sequence Numbers (DSN) to avoid counting to infinity that is why it is loop free. This is the characteristic of this algorithm. When a node send request to a destination, it sends its DSNs together with all routing information. It also selects the most favorable route based on the sequence number [15]

In this paper explains regarding to Ad hoc Networks Security Strategy based on Routing Protocols. So the now a day's security issue is the major problem in wireless network. And when we talking about the different attacks the most destructive attacks in the wireless network is wormhole attacks. In this two or more malicious colluding nodes create higher level virtual tunnels in the n/w. This tunnel follows the shortest link in the n/w in which the records transmitted the packet at one node to other in the n/w. Our main focus on the paper is to analyze the performance of reactive multicast routing protocol On Demand Multicasting Protocol under the control of worm hole nodes with differ design. The proposed protocol reduces the packet loss due to malicious nodes to a considerable extent thereby enhancing the performance. In this paper also described using UDP (user datagram protocol) packets, the source to destination route is discovered and maintain by these messages. For example the node which request, will use its IP address as Originator IP address for the message for broadcast. It simply means that the AODV not blindly forwarded every message. The number of hops of routing messages in ad hoc network is determined by Time-To-Live (TTL) in the IP header. [16]

In this book of Routing protocols and concepts, CCNA exploration companion guide. "Introduction to dynamic routing protocols" clearly described about routing means to choose a path. Routing in MANET means to choose a right and suitable path from source to destination. Routing terminology is used in different kinds of networks such as in telephony technology, electronic data networks and in the internet network. Here work is more concern about routing in mobile ad hoc networks. Protocols are the set of rules through which two or more devices (mobile nodes, computers or electronic devices) can communicate to each other. In mobile ad hoc networks the routing is mostly done with the help of routing tables. These tables are kept in the memory cache of these mobile nodes. When routing process is going on, it route the data packets in different mechanisms. The first is unicast, in which the source directly sends the data packets to the destination. The sec is multicast, in this the source node sends data packet to the specified multiple nodes in the network. Exchanging information between these dynamic routers learn to know about the new routes and networks. Dynamic routing is more flexible than static routing. In dynamic routing it have the capability to overcome the overload traffic. Dynamic routing uses different paths to forward the data packets. Dynamic routing is better than static routing. [19]

This survey paper of "Research on Intrusion Detection and Response: A Survey" provides a review of an intrusion detection to gather with a study on technologies implemented by some researchers in this research area. Honey pots are one of the effective detection tools to sense attacks such as port or email scanning activities in the network. Some features and applications of honey pots are explained in this paper. Main goal of that paper is to review the current trends in ID Systems (IDS) and to analyzing some of the current problems that exist in this research area. The current trend for the IDS is far from a reliable protective system, but instead the main idea is to make it possible to detect novel network attacks. One of the main parts is to make sure that in case of an intrusion attempt, the system is able to detect and to report it. Once the detection is reliable, next step would be to protect the network (response). [21]

In This Research discussing about the" Importance of Intrusion Detection System (IDS)" IDS is a new technology of the mechanism for intrusion detection methods that have come out in recent past years. Intrusion detection system's performed important role in a network is to help computer systems to prepare and deal with the different network attacks. IDS is also very useful for the monitoring and analyze both user and system activities, Analyze the system configurations and Vulnerabilities, Assessing system and file integrity, Ability to recognize patterns typical of different attacks, Analysis of abnormal activity patterns, Tracking the user policy violations.[22]

Intrusion detection is to monitoring on the network resources to detect anomalous behavior and misuse in network. This concept has been around for nearly about twenty years but only recently has it seen a dramatic rise in popularity and incorporation into the overall information security infrastructure. Beginning in 1980, with James Anderson's paper, Computer Security Threat Monitoring and Surveillance, the intrusion detection was born. Since then, several polar events in IDS technology have advanced intrusion detection to its current state. [22]

In this research they discussing about the "Analysis of wormhole intrusion attacks in MANET". A wormhole is an attack in the routing protocol based on Mobile Ad-hoc Network (MANET). In a wormhole attack, two or more active nodes create a sequence that two remote region of a Mobile Adhoc Network are directly connected through nodes that exist to be neighbors but actually distant from one another. This shortcut is created by connecting the purported neighbors through a covert communication channel. A wormhole thus also allows an attacker to create two attacker-controlled choke points which can be utilized by the attacker to degrade or analyze traffic at a desired time. Our focus in this paper is a particular form of the wormhole attack called the self contained in-band wormhole. [23]

In this research paper we have described some of the basic routing protocols in mobile adhoc network like Destination Sequenced Distance Vector, Dynamic Source Routing, Temporally-Ordered Routing Algorithm and Ad-hoc On Demand Distance Vector. Security is a one of the huge issue in MANETs as they are infrastructure-less and autonomous. Main goal of writing this paper is to address some basic security concerns in mobile adhoc network, operation in wormhole attacks and securing the well-known routing protocol Ad-hoc On Demand Distance Vector. This article is very useful for the people who work in the real world problems in MANET security. [24]

Mobile Ad-hoc Network (MANET) is a set of various wireless mobile nodes without fixed network infrastructure and centralized administration. In communication done through in MANET is via multi-hop paths. In mobile adhoc network there are lots of challenges because of its large area. MANET contains diverse resources, the line of defence is very unclear, in MANET Nodes operate in shared wireless medium, network topology changes unpredictably and very dynamically, one of the issue is radio link reliability, connection breaks are pretty frequent. Moreover, destination of nodes, number of nodes and mobility of these hosts may vary in different applications. There is no stationary infrastructure. Each node in MANET acts a router that forwards data packets to other node. [24]

In this paper of "A Review on: Detection and Prevention of wormhole attacks in MANET" Wormhole Attack in Manet is one of the cruellest attacks on routing protocols in which two or more malicious nodes receive packets at one point of the network and transmit them to another location by a wired or wireless tunnel. This attack is very powerful and that the detection of it is very difficult work. This attack is a one kind of a serious threat in wireless networks, especially against many wireless ad-hoc networks and location-based wireless security systems. There is several wormhole detection and Prevention methods in the wireless ad-hoc networks some of them are described in this article. There are some of the technique are define here Distance and location Based: Packet Leash Technique, Special Hardware Based Approaches, Localized Encryption and Authentication Protocol (LEAP), Topological Technique, Watchdog Technique, DelPHI Technique [25]

Chapter 3
PRESENT WORK

This Chapter Contains about the Present Work about the Present Paper and the Problem definition, future scope of the technique, objectives about the work and what is your motive about this technology, which tools and technology apply in this present work this all this things are in this chapter.

3.1 Scope of Study

We have lots of technique to reduce the attacks over the internet environment for example hardware firewall or software firewall but some attacks or some of the   proxy software can also enter in our network. As Intrusion Detection System is used as second line of defense to identify the attacks on the networks as well as on the host machine. Intrusion Detection System has the efficiency to detect malicious activity and report it to the user. When IDS not capable to identify all the attacks in that cases the developer of the IDS make the security rules tighter than previous one. Due to these tighter rules sometimes IDS alarms unnecessarily. Actually these are false positive alarms. So no need to alert the user while such type of sign is found by IDS. In other case if the developer looses the security rule than it may happen some true attacks are not identified by the IDS. Due to the inherent limitations of the IDSs we have to filter the false alarms from the system.

3.2 Problem formulation

Now a day's Intrusion detection is one of the popular technique for the any of the organization to secure and safe his data over the unauthenticated person or misuses or the hackers among the network. Intrusion Detection System at present generally applied in the routing layer as a network layer so the traffic is much more and speed and accuracy is not there or And IDS algorithms is not so secure so we plan to investigate more attack scenarios in MANETs, not only at the routing layer, but also at MAC Layer. Analysis of the threats could help to construct more security-related features and misuse based intrusion detection systems. This, in turn, will help us design better aggregation and correlation algorithms [3] Bo Sun & Kui Wu & Udo W. Pooch "Zone-Based Intrusion Detection for Mobile Ad Hoc Networks"

3.3 Objectives

- The main important purpose is to reduce the attacks on the network.
- To reduce the traffic over the network to provide a speed and accuracy over the network to applying in IDS in not in the routing layer but in the transport layer.
- Most of the people use internet in their day to day life. For example- now we can transfer data from one place to another with the help of internet. Sometimes it may be some secure information. If some unauthorized user disclose it in the middle than it will be a problem.
- For another example while we do financial transaction with the help of internet. Than security is a primary concern. To secure network with speedily and accurately in the other layer of OSI is the primary aim.

Chapter 4
RESEARCH METODOLOGY

In this research we used the simulation environment for the mobile adhoc network because it is very hard to watch the result in real time environment or need so many devices or it is also very costly so here all work will apply in the simulator and that is the NS-2. And NS-2 is work on the Linux so we have also installed the Linux operating system that is ubuntu as well.

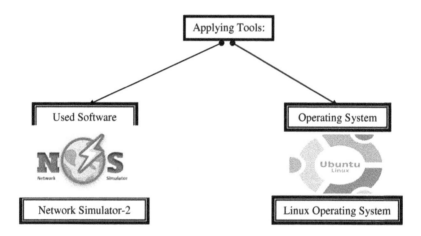

Figure 4.1 Tools Used

Network simulator 2 is the tool in which we apply for networking research. NS-2 is a standard experiment environment in research community. Provide substantial support to simulate bunch of protocols like TCP, UDP, FTP, HTTP and DSR.

Figure 4.2 Real Life Environments [5]

Figure 4.3 Simulated Environments [5]

Chapter 5
RESULT AND DISCUSSION

In this research work first of all we introduced the one attack that is wormhole attack whenever they try to attacking in the network nodes the intrusion detection system can activated automatically at the same time and through this intrusion detection system administrator can also knowing about that attacks through the snorts IDS in mobile adhoc network. In this system packet drops concept also used when the wormhole attacks can happen in the network node. Whole work can done in the Media Access Control layer. Main purpose of the IDS apply in the mac layer is to early detection of any of the attacks or viruses then the routing network layer.

Actually in this research mainly two file created one is test_IDS.tcl file and the rest one is IDS.nam file. In tcl file contains the coding part of the research work and the nam file contains the output or demo of this research work. Now let we see the step by step results screen shot with its explanation with whole process of this research.

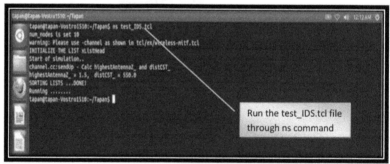

Figure 5.1 Compile the TCL File Successfully

In this snapshot run the test_IDS.tcl file that is running correctly as u see in the above screen.

Figure 5.2 Screen Shot of Run Time Screen

In this second screen shot run the nam file through the nam commands to display the two file on the screen one is simulation demo files and rest one is the nam info file. In the simulated demo file when u click on the play button the your research work is start now.

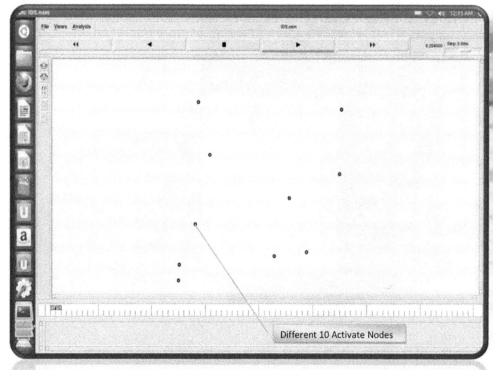

Figure 5.3 Screen Shot Simulation Work with 10 Activate Nodes

Mainly in our work is on the mobile adhoc network so that is always depending on the different kind of the nodes which are also known as the particular system or mobile device. In this screen shot when we click on the play button the demonstration can start automatically and generates the 10 activate nodes in mobile adhoc networks

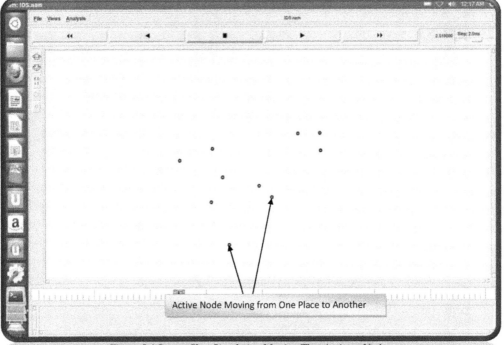

Figure 5.4 Screen Shot Simulation Moving That Activate Nodes

In this screen shot the activate node moving around the network at one place to another place because of its characteristic. Mobile node is not static it dynamically changes his topology. In first snapshot the node place is differ then this snap shot as u see clearly on this snap shot.

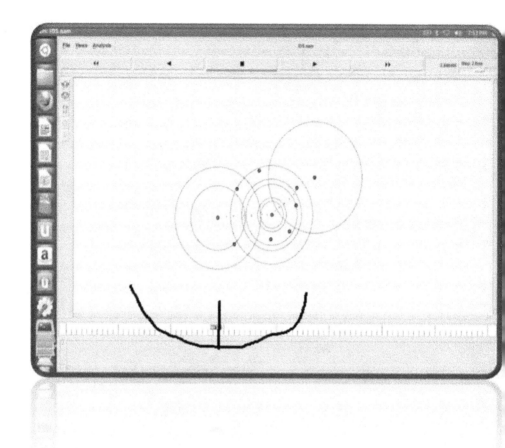

tunneling between the node 4, node 5, node 6. At The Same time the intrusion detection system is also automatically generates and detect that wormhole attacks.

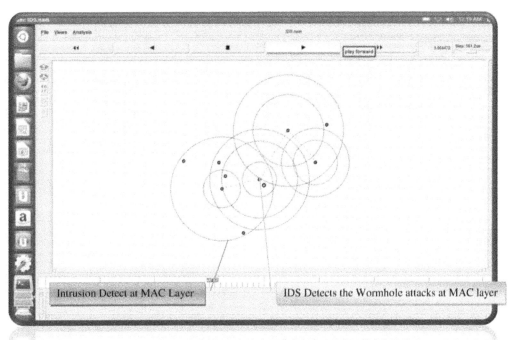

Figure 5.6 Screen Shot Simulation of Automatic Activate Of IDS

In this scenario when the intrusion detection system detect the wormhole attacks the intrusion detection system will automatically activated and take the action as well this whole work done in the MAC layer.

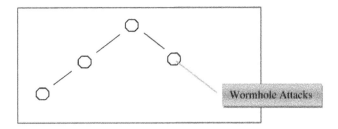

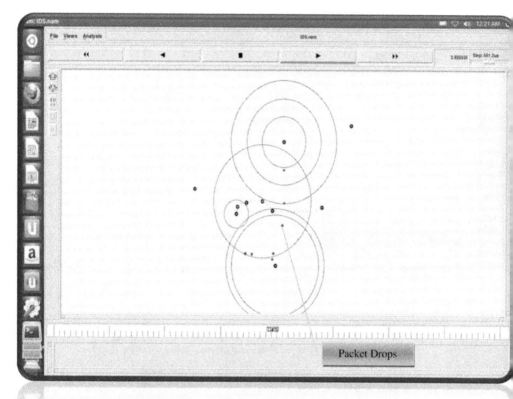

Figure 5.7 Screen Shot of Packet Dropping

In above screen shot the wormhole attacks through the some of the packets also drops in the networks above blue color rectangle is a sign of the packet drops.

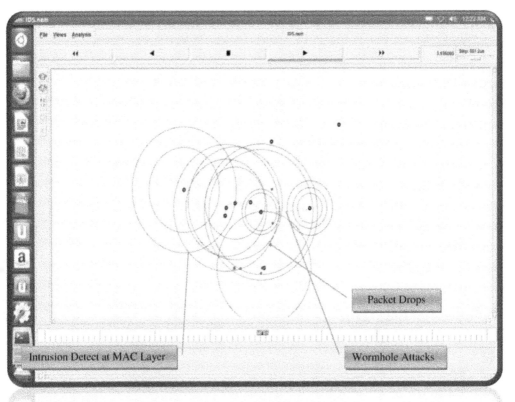

Figure 5.8 IDS Tried To Solved the Problem

In this snap shot the intrusion detection system is detects whole malicious node affected through the wormhole attacks and also trying to recover the packets whose effected from wormhole attacks. As u see IDS is continuously working and gave the best performance.

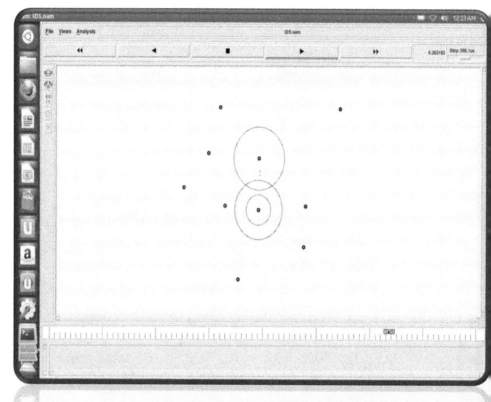

Figure 5.9 Wormhole Attack Effect Decreases

In this snapshot you see the demonstration finally at the end point. The wormhole attacks can decreases and effect of that attacks can also decreases and intrusion detection system is finally detect most of the malicious node as well as the effected node.

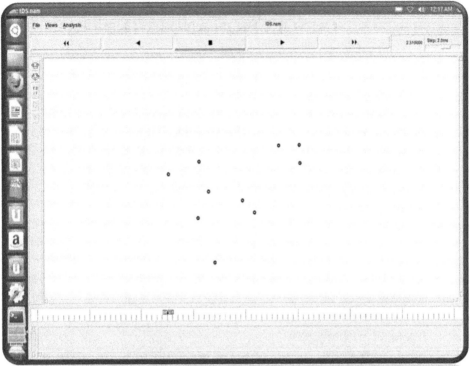

Figure 5.10 Screen Shot of All Mobile Nodes Is In Normal Mode

Finally the all 10 nodes are coming in the normal moving mode, Intrusion can detect at the mac layer in mobile adhoc network through the applying the wormhole attacks.

Chapter 6
CONCLUSION AND FUTUREWORK

5.1 Conclusion

In this research work we proposed the Intrusion detection system which is basically works on the network routing layer but here we first introduced the wormhole attacks and then that Intrusion detection system detect that attacks is in the Media Access Control Layer (MAC) main purpose of that research is for the early detection of the different kinds of attacks and workload can also decrease of the network layer so network layer can also doing other task easily.

5.2 Future Work

Mobile adhoc network is very large area and its work on so many different place like a military area for the purpose of defense, at medical emergency system, at banking or other so many places so there is no much as security attacks can happen any time at any kind of like denial of services attacks wormhole attacks, black hole attacks, gray hole attacks for the data traffic attacks.

So here we apply Intrusion Detection System at in the media access control layer for the one particular wormhole attacks but we also apply intrusion detection system at the different kind of attacks for the different security purpose or we can also apply one or more attacks at the same time detects by intrusion detection system at the mac layer for the early detection.

Chapter 7

REFERENCES AND BIBLIOGRAPHY

Research Papers

[1] Prof. Radha S. Shirbhate & Prof. Pallavi A. Patil (Jan 2012) *"Network Traffic Monitoring Using Intrusion Detection System"*, IEEE transactions on software engineering Volume 2, Issue 1, ISSN: 2277 128X

[2] Dorothy E. Denning (1987) *"An intrusion detection model"*, IEEE transactions on software engineering vol. se 13 number-2

[3] Bo Sun, Kui Wu, Udo W. Pooch, *"Zone-Based Intrusion Detection for Mobile Ad Hoc Networks"*, Journal on Adhoc Networks in gurd conference, Vol.10, No. 7, pp 1179-1190, March 2010.

[4] Tiranuch Anantvalee (Department of Computer Science and Engineering Florida Atlantic University, Boca Raton, FL 33428) Jie Wu (Department of Computer Science and Engineering Florida Atlantic University, Boca Raton, FL 33428) 2006 *"A Survey on Intrusion Detection in Mobile Ad Hoc Networks"*, Wireless/Mobile Network Security 2006 Springer

[5] Chin-Yang Henry Tseng M.S. (Santa Clara University) 2002 B.A. (National Chiao-Tung University, Taiwan) 1998 *"Distributed Intrusion Detection Models for Mobile Ad Hoc Networks"*, PHD Thesis Paper

[6] S.Madhavi (Research Scholar, Dept of Computer, Science & Engineering, Acharya Nagarjuna University, India.), Dr. Tai Hoon Kim, (Professor, Dept. of Multimedia, Hannam University, Korea.) July 2008 *"An Intrusion Detection System in Mobile Ad hoc Network"*, International Journal of Security and Its Applications Vol. 2, No.3

[7] Sevil S»en, John A. Clark, and Juan E. Tapiador (Department of Computer Science, University of York, YO10 5DD, UK) *"Power-Aware Intrusion Detection in Mobile Ad Hoc Networks"*

[8] A. Abraham, C. Grosan, and C. Martiv-Vide (2007) *"Evolutionary design of Intrusion Detection Programs"*, Int. Journal of Network Security, 4:328-339

[9] Yuxin meng and lam-for kwok (2011) *"Adaptive false alarm filter using machine learning in intrusion detection"*, computer science department city university of hong kong , hong kong china springer-verlag barlin Heidelberg pp 573-584

[10] Loukas Lazos, and Marwan Krunz, *"Selective Jamming/Dropping Insider Attacks in Wireless Mesh Networks"* An International Journal on Engineering Science and Technology Arizona edu, Vol.2, No. 2, pp 265-269, April 2010.

[11] Ajay Prakash Rai, Vineet Srivastava, Rinkoo Bhatia, *"Wormhole Attack Detection in Mobile Ad Hoc Networks"*, International Journal of Engineering and Innovative Technology, Vol.2, No. 2, pp 384-389, August 2012.

[12] R.Vidhya, G. P. Ramesh Kumar, *"Securing Data in Ad hoc Networks using Multipath routing"*, International Journal of Advances in Engineering & Technology, Vol.1, No. 5, pp 337-341, November 2011.

[13] K.Kiruthika Devi, M.Ravichandran, *"Detecting Sinking Behavior at MAC and Network Layer Using SVM in Wireless Ad hoc Networks"*, International Journal of Computer Science and Network (IJCSN), Vol. 1, Issue. 3, pp. 12-16, June 2012.

[14] Turgay Korkmaz, *"Verifying Physical Presence of Neighbors against Replay-based Attacks in Wireless Ad Hoc Networks"*, Information Technology: Coding and Computing, International Journal of Information Technology , Vol. 2, No. 2, pp 704-709, April 2005.

[15] Van Phuong T., Ngo Trong Canh, Young-Koo Lee, Sungyoung Lee, Heejo Lee, " *Transmission Time-based Mechanism to Detect Wormhole Attacks"*, IEEE Conference on Asia-Pacific Service Computing Conference, pp 172- 178, December 2007.

[16] Ma Hongwei, *"The Study on Ad hoc Networks Security Strategy based on Routing Protocols"*, IEEE International Conference on Computer Science and Network Technology, Vol.1, No.4, pp 445-449, December 2011.

[17] E.A.Mary Anita, V.Thulasi Bai, E.L.Kiran Raj, B.Prabhu, *"Defending against Worm Hole Attacks in Multicast Routing Protocols for Mobile Ad hoc Networks"* IEEE International Conference on Information Theory and Aerospace & Electronics Systems Technology, pp 1–5, March 2011.

[18] Scarfone, K., Mell, P.: *Guide to Intrusion Detection and Prevention System*, pp.800-894. NIST special publication (2007)

[19] Routing protocols and concepts, CCNA exploration companion guide. *"Introduction to dynamic routing protocols"*. Chapter three, pp 148-177.

[20] Saleh Ali K.Al-Omari, Putra Sumari *"An overview of mobile adhoc networks for the existing protocols and applications"* Journal of applications of graph theory in wireless adhoc network and sensor network(J Graph-Hoc), March 2010

[21] Peyman Kabiri , Ali A. Ghorbani," *Research on Intrusion Detection and Response: A Survey*", International Journal of Network Security, Vol.1, No.2, PP.84–102, Sep. 2005

[22] Asmaa Shaker Ashoor, Prof. Sharad Gore," Importance of Intrusion Detection System (IDS)" International Journal of Scientific & Engineering Research, Volume 2, Issue 1, January-2011 1 ISSN 2229-5518

[23] Viren Mahajan, Maitreya Natu, Adarshpal Sethi," *Analysis of wormhole intrusion attacks in MANET*", University of Delaware, mahajan@cis.udel.edu

[24] Rutvij H. Jhaveri1, Ashish D. Patel, Jatin D. Parmar, Bhavin I. Shah, "*MANET Routing Protocols and Wormhole Attack against AODV*", IJCSNS International Journal of Computer Science and Network Security, VOL.10 No.4, April 2010

[25] Yashpalsinh Gohil, Sumegha Sakhreliya, Sumitra Menaria, "*A Review on: Detection and Prevension of wormhole attacks in MANET*", International Journal of Scientific and Research Publications, Volume 3, Issue 2, February 2013 1 ISSN 2250-3153

[26] Loukas Lazos, and Marwan Krunz, "Selective Jamming/Dropping Insider Attacks in Wireless Mesh Networks" An International Journal on Engineering
Science and Technology Arizona edu, Vol.2, No. 2, pp 265-269, April 2010.

[27] Ajay Prakash Rai, Vineet Srivastava, Rinkoo Bhatia, "Wormhole Attack Detection in Mobile Ad Hoc Networks", International Journal of Engineering and Innovative Technology, Vol.2, No. 2, pp 384-389, August 2012.   [4] Routing protocols and concepts, CCNA exploration companion guide. „„Introduction to dynamic routing protocols"". Chapter three, pp 148-177.

[28] R.Vidhya, G. P. Ramesh Kumar, "Securing Data in Ad hoc Networks using Multipath routing", International Journal of Advances in Engineering & Technology, Vol.1, No. 5, pp 337-341, November 2011.

[29] K.Kiruthika Devi, M.Ravichandran, "Detecting Sinking Behavior at MAC and Network Layer Using SVM in Wireless Ad hoc Networks, International Journal of Computer Science and Network (IJCSN), Vol. 1, Issue. 3, pp. 12-16,June 2012.

[30] Turgay Korkmaz, "Verifying Physical Presence of Neighbors against Replay-based Attacks in Wireless Ad Hoc Networks", Information Technology: Coding and Computing, International Journal of Information Technology , Vol. 2, No. 2, pp 704-709, April 2005.

[31] Van Phuong T., Ngo Trong Canh, Young-Koo Lee, Sungyoung Lee, Heejo Lee, " Transmission Time- based Mechanism to Detect Wormhole Attacks", IEEE Conference on Asia-Pacific Service Computing Conference, pp 172- 178, December 2007.

[32] Ma Hongwei, "The Study on Ad hoc Networks Security Strategy based on Routing Protocols", IEEE International Conference on Computer Science and Network Technology, Vol.1, No.4, pp 445-449, December 2011.

[33] E.A.Mary Anita, V.Thulasi Bai, E.L.Kiran Raj, B.Prabhu, "Defending against Worm Hole Attacks in Multicast Routing Protocols for Mobile Ad hoc Networks" IEEE International Conference on Information Theory and Aerospace & Electronics Systems Technology, pp 1–5, March 2011.

[34] Tapan P. Gondaliya, Maninder Singh, Lovely Professional University "Intrusion detection System for Attack Prevention in Mobile Ad-hoc Network", Volume 3, Issue 4, April 2013.

[35] Tapan P. Gondaliya, Maninder Singh, Lovely Professional University "Intrusion Detection System on MAC Layer for Attack Prevention in MANET", ICCENT 2013, IEEE Explore Journal, ISBN: 978-1-4799-3925-1

[36]   Nitin Mohan Sharma, Tapan P Gondaliya, "Enhance IDS False Alarm Filtering Using KNN Classifier", International Journal of Emerging Research in Management &Technology ISSN: 2278-9359 Volume- 2, Issue-5, May 2013

[37] Nitin Mohan Sharma, Kunwar Pal, "Implementation of decision tree algorithm after clustering Through WEKA" International Journal of Computer Engineering and Technology (IJCET), Volume 4, Issue 1, Jan. – Feb. 2013 pp. 358-363 Published by IAEME

Web Sites

[1] http://www.symantec.com/connect/articles/introduction-ids

[2] http://www.intrusion-detection-system-group.co.uk/

[3] http://en.wikipedia.org

[4] http://packetstormsecurity.org/papers/wireless/

[5] http://www.google.com

[6] http:/www.google.com/images

YOUR KNOWLEDGE HAS VALUE

- We will publish your bachelor's and
  master's thesis, essays and papers

- Your own eBook and book -
  sold worldwide in all relevant shops

- Earn money with each sale

Upload your text at www.GRIN.com
and publish for free